Sound at Sight

oboe

Grades 1-8

by James Rae

Published by
Trinity College London Press Ltd
trinitycollege.com

Registered in England
Company no. 09726123

Printed in England by Caligraving Ltd

• Grade 1

Count one-beat, two-beat and four-beat notes carefully. Remember to check the dynamics before you begin.

11

12

• # Grade 2

The $\frac{3}{4}$ time signature is introduced, along with simple ties and slurs.

1

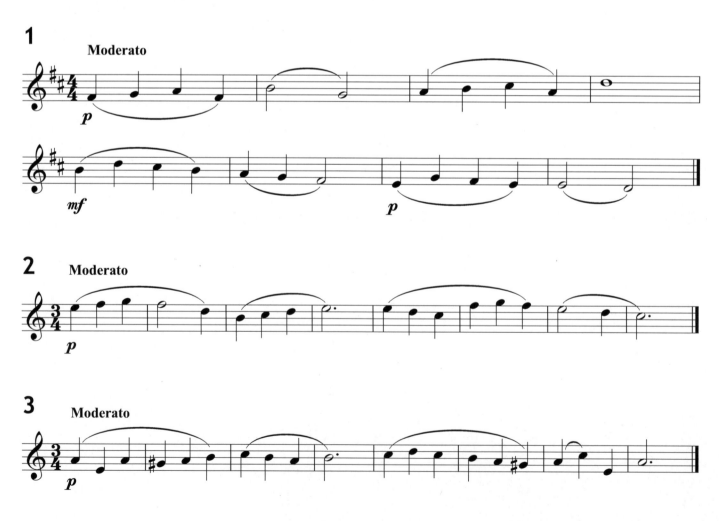

2

3

9

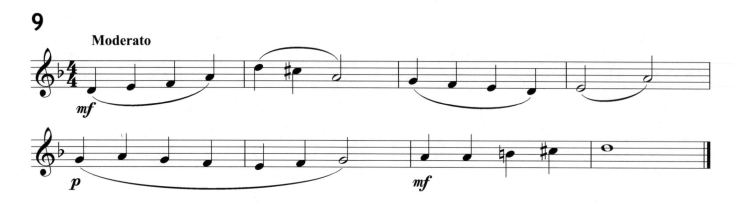

10

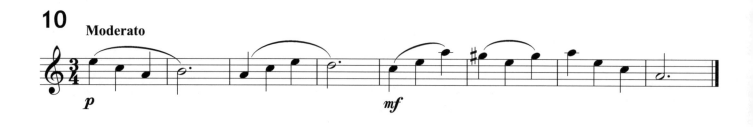

11

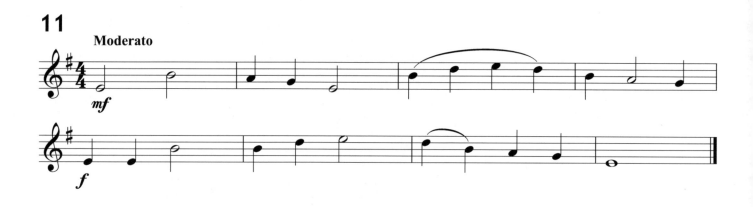

12

Grade 3

Quavers are included at this grade. Andante means 'walking pace'.

5 Allegretto

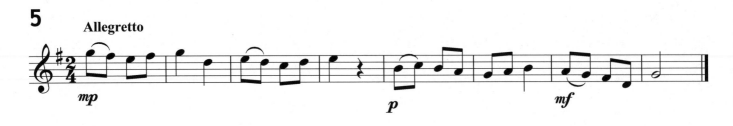

6 Andante

7 Andante

8 Allegretto

9 Allegretto

10 Andante

11

12

• Grade 4

Staccato notes are added at this grade in addition to *crescendo* (*cresc.*) and *diminuendo* (*dim.*).

1

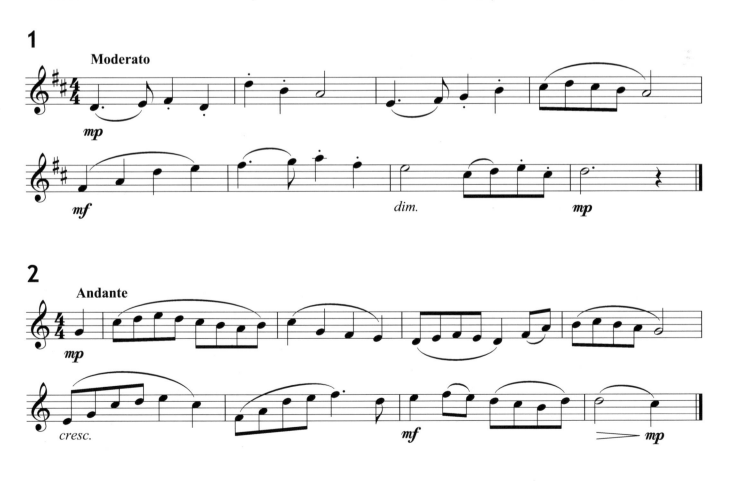

2

7 Moderato

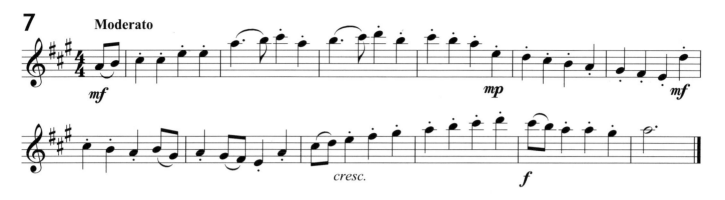

8 Allegretto

9 Allegretto

10 Andante

11

12

- # Grade 5

  Semiquavers and the $\frac{6}{8}$ time signature are introduced at Grade 5.

1

Grade 6

$\frac{3}{8}$ and dotted notes are featured at Grade 6.

4

5

6

7 **Slow rock**

8 **Moderate waltz tempo**

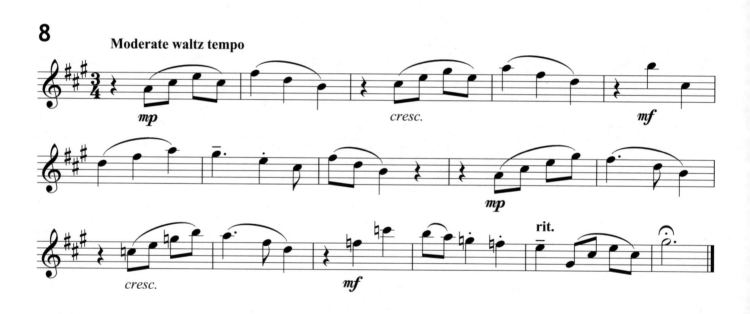

Grade 7

Triplets are introduced at this grade, along with accelerandos and the $\frac{9}{8}$ time signature.

• Grade 8

Changing time signatures and duplets may be included at Grade 8.

4